GW00400855

G. F. HANDEL

The complete sonatas

for treble (alto) recorder and basso continuo

Die gesamten Sonaten

für Altblockflöte und basso continuo

*edited from all the autograph manuscripts
and other contemporary sources by*

*herausgegeben unter Benutzung aller
autographen Manuskripte und anderer
zeitgenössischer Quellen von*

DAVID LASOCKI
and
WALTER BERGMANN

1979
FABER MUSIC LIMITED
London

© 1979 by Faber Music Ltd
First published in 1979 by Faber Music Ltd
3 Queen Square London WC1N 3AU
Cover design by Shirley Tucker
Printed in England
All rights reserved

The cover portrait of Handel by Thomas Hudson
is from the Mansell Collection

CONTENTS

PREFACE

Why another edition of the Handel recorder sonatas? Briefly, because these sonatas, among the best loved and most frequently performed of all works for the instrument, have never been presented in any edition that fully reflects the composer's intentions. The autograph manuscripts of three of the six sonatas, as well as significant copyists' manuscripts of five of the sonatas, have been completely overlooked, and there has therefore also been no proper evaluation of the sources. The principal sources for four of the sonatas have always been the early printed editions, which seem to have been unauthorised by Handel and can now be seen to contain notable departures from his own manuscripts. Furthermore, a full survey has never been made of the concordances of the movements from the sonatas – the uses to which Handel put them in later compositions – although such a survey turns out to shed light on many details of the sonatas themselves.

The present edition is therefore an attempt to present these six recorder sonatas as the composer intended them. Full details and a discussion of the sources, concordances, a discussion of other recorder sonatas attributed to Handel, and a complete listing of all the differences among the sources may be found in the Critical Report at the end of this edition. It should only be mentioned that the variant readings of certain passages found at the bottom of the pages in question (the most significant readings from secondary or alternative primary sources) are those which we felt all performers would wish to know about, especially because in many cases they represent the text as it is generally known and performed. (For the meaning of the identifying letters *M, R, S* and *W,* see the Critical Report.)

All editorial markings are distinguished from the original text by means of brackets and dotted slurs. We have added editorial appoggiaturas at cadential trills where the bass figures demand them (their performed length is left to the taste of the player). Where appoggiaturas are not indicated by the composer or the editors, their performance is at the discretion of the performer. We should only mention that in our opinion Handel made an intentional distinction in the bass figures between cadences where he wanted a long appoggiatura and cadences where he wanted

a short or no appoggiatura. We have added some editorial slurs where we thought them essential, usually by analogy with other passages in the same movement; the addition of other slurs by the performer is by no means excluded. We have also added editorial trills at cadences. Accidentals in brackets before a note are editorial suggestions for an alteration of the composer's text; accidentals in brackets above notes are precautionary.

The basso continuo can be played on any kind of keyboard instrument, lute, guitar, etc. The addition of a violoncello or viola da gamba is useful when the instrument used for accompanying the recorder is weak in the bass register; it should double the bass line, although rapid figuration (as, for example, in the second movement of the A minor sonata) should preferably be played by only one of the instruments.

In the present edition the basso continuo has been realised by the editors from the figured bass line as they think the composer might have conceived it. We have aimed at appropriate style and balance with and subordination to the recorder part, and tried to avoid musical and technical dullness. The idea that a basso continuo accompaniment must be improvised is historically incorrect; such a realisation can and should be carefully prepared. It matters a great deal what is played as well as how it is played. In a few cases where the bass figures seem to be wrong or doubtful, our realisation has by-passed them, although the figures have not been altered. At cadences the player will have to adjust the harmonisation to what the soloist plays, whether a long or short appoggiatura or none at all. The basso continuo player may accordingly play a 6/4, 3/4, 5/4 or 6/5 chord, or leave out the dissonant note, as the situation demands; in such cases the bass figures and their realisation by the editors are over-ridden.

The present edition is published by permission of the Syndics of the Fitzwilliam Museum and of the Cultural Committee of the City of Manchester, to both of whom we are most grateful. We should also like to acknowledge the very great help given to us during the preparation of the edition by Terence Best, The Hon. Gerald Coke, Edgar Hunt, Betty Bang Mather and Guy Oldham.

DAVID LASOCKI
WALTER BERGMANN
London, October 1978

VORWORT

Der Grund, warum hiermit eine neue Ausgabe von Händels Blockflötensonaten vorgelegt wird, ist kurz gesagt der, dass diese meist geliebten und unter allen Blockflötensonaten am häufigsten gespielten Sonaten bisher noch niemals in einer Ausgabe erschienen sind, die Händels Intentionen voll gerecht wurde. Die autographen Manuskripte von drei, sowie wesentliche handschriftliche Kopien von fünf der sechs Sonaten waren vollständig übersehen worden; auch liess die Bewertung der Quellen viel zu wünschen übrig. Stets waren die Hauptquellen von vier Sonaten frühe Drucke, die, wie es scheint, ohne Händels Autorisation erschienen waren und die, wie wir heute sehen können, beachtenswerte Abweichungen von seinen eigenen Manuskripten enthalten. Hinzu kommt, dass noch niemals eine vollständige vergleichende Übersicht über die Sätze gemacht worden war, die Händel später für andere Kompositionen benutzte, obwohl eine solche Übersicht viele Einzelheiten in den Sonaten selbst beleuchtet.

Die vorliegende Ausgabe dient daher dem Zweck, diese sechs Blockflötensonaten so darzubieten, wie der Komponist es beabsichtigte. Alle Einzelheiten, eine Besprechung der Quellen, Konkordanzen, die Erörterung anderer Händel zugeschriebener Blockflötensonaten und eine vollständige Liste aller Verschiedenheiten innerhalb der Quellen finden sich im *Critical Report* am Ende dieser Ausgabe. Hier sei nur bemerkt, dass die abweichenden Lesarten gewisser Stellen (aus erst- und zweitklassigen Quellen), die als Fussnoten im vorliegenden Druck erscheinen, diejenigen sind, über die sich alle Spieler sicherlich orientieren wollen, da sie in vielen Fällen einen Text darstellen, der allgemein bekannt ist und allgemein gespielt wird. (Die Bedeutung der Buchstaben *M, R, S* und *W* geht aus dem *Critical Report* hervor.)

Alle Zeichen der Herausgeber sind durch Klammern und gestrichelte Bögen vom Originaltext unterschieden. Vorhalte vor Kadenztrillern wurden zugesetzt, wo die Bassziffern es verlangten; ihre Länge ist dem Geschmack des Spielers überlassen. Weitere Vorhalte, weder vom Komponisten verlangt noch von den Herausgebern vorgeschlagen, stehen im Ermessen des Spielers. Es scheint, dass Händel einen bewussten Unterschied in der Bass-beziferung von Kadenzen machte, wo er einen langen oder kurzen Vorhalt verlangt. Bindebögen in Analogie zu gleichen Stellen im selben Satz wurden zugefügt; es steht dem Spieler frei, weitere Bindungen zu machen. Kadenztriller wurden ebenfalls ergänzt. Eingeklammerte Vorzeichen *vor* den Noten sind Vorschläge der Herausgeber, *über* den Noten Bestätigungen.

Die basso continuo Begleitung kann auf jedem Tasteninstrument, auf Laute, Gitarre usw. gespielt werden. Wenn das Begleitinstrument im Bassregister schwach ist, kann ein Violoncello oder eine Viola da Gamba die Basslinie verdoppeln; schnelle Passagen (z. Bsp. im zweiten Satz der A moll Sonate) sollten dagegen vorzugsweise nur auf dem einen oder dem andern Instrument gespielt werden.

Der basso continuo der vorliegenden Sonaten ist von den Herausgebern so ausgesetzt wie sie denken, dass der Komponist ihn gespielt wissen wollte. Das Ziel war: Stil, Ausgewogenheit mit der Blockflötenstimme und Unterordnung unter sie bei Vermeidung musikalischer und technischer Langeweile. Die Idee, dass eine basso continuo Begleitung improvisiert werden müsse, ist historisch nicht haltbar; die Begleitung kann und sollte gut vorbereitet werden. Es kommt darauf an, was gespielt wird, nicht nur wie. Wo die Bassziffern nicht zu stimmen scheinen, sind die Herausgeber von ihnen abgewichen ohne jedoch die Ziffern zu verändern. Bei Kadenzen muss der Begleiter die Harmonien dem anpassen, was der Blockflötenspieler spielt: einen langen oder kurzen Vorhalt oder garkeinen. Er muss demgemäss einen 6/4, 3/4, 5/4 oder 6/5 Akkord greifen oder die dissonierende Note auslassen, wie es die Situation erfordert; in solchen Fällen muss er von der Bezifferung und ihrer Aussetzung durch die Herausgeber abweichen.

Die vorliegende Ausgabe erscheint mit der Erlaubnis der Syndics des Fitzwilliam Museums in Cambridge und des Cultural Committee der Stadt Manchester, denen beiden die Herausgeber zu Dank verpflichtet sind. Sie danken gleichfalls Mr. Terence Best, The Hon. Gerald Coke, Mr. Edgar Hunt, Prof. Betty Bang Mather und Mr. Guy Oldham für die grosse Hilfe bei der Vorbereitung der vorliegenden Ausgabe.

David Lasocki
Walter Bergmann
London, October 1978

PREFACE TO THE SECOND EDITION

Since the publication of this edition, new research by several Handel scholars into the types of paper he used for his manuscripts has indicated later dates than we suggested for the autograph manuscripts of the recorder sonatas.[1] Moreover, another Handel scholar has brought to light the purpose for which the fair copies of four of the sonatas were made and the reason why they were unknown to the publisher Walsh.

The autographs of the recorder sonatas are written on two different types of paper. First, the manuscripts of the Bb major and D minor sonatas are written on some Italian paper of a type that Handel used for other works composed between December 1724 and early 1726. Among those other works are the drafts of some thoroughbass exercises that were intended for the instruction either of Princess Anne, the daughter of George II, to whom Handel had become music master by 1724, or – more likely, since they ended up in his own collection – of John Christopher Smith junior, the son of Handel's amanuensis and principal copyist, whom he began teaching in 1725. The writing of the Bb sonata in particular is very similar to that of these exercises. Handel probably did not, as we suggested (Critical Report, p. 69), acquire this paper on his early travels in Italy but obtained it much later from some as yet unknown source.

Second, the fair copies of the G minor, A minor, C major and F major sonatas as well as the drafts of the sixth and seventh movements of the D minor sonata are written on some Dutch paper of a type that Handel used for other works composed between December 1725 and April 1726. Among those works are fair copies of both the thoroughbass exercises referred to above and some exercises in fugal composition intended for the same purpose. Alfred Mann has recently pointed out that 'in general appearance, and with their decorative headings' the fair copies of the four recorder sonatas 'very much resemble the various fair copies' of Handel's instructional exercises.[2] Indeed, he believes the recorder sonatas to have been 'an integral part of Handel's thoroughbass instruction', the chief argument being 'the unusually conscientious notation of figured bass symbols. Among various similar autographs in the Fitzwilliam Collection, the one most easily compared to the autographs of the recorder sonatas is that of the A major violin sonata

Op. 1 no. 3 . . . Yet this work – as well as other sonatas of the collection – appears without any figures in the continuo part'.[3] The instructional purpose for the autographs in fact 'may be the reason to which posterity owes their remarkably good condition: they were executed and preserved in exemplary manner. Even in the earliest lessons Handel's fair copies could not have posed any reading difficulties for the pupil'.[4] It also suggests why the manuscripts should have been unknown to Walsh: they were special copies made for private use.

In the light of the new dating of the paper on which the recorder sonatas were written, let us re-examine the evidence for their dates of composition. First, the Bb major sonata, written in a corrected draft on paper Handel used between December 1724 and early 1726, has handwriting that closely resembles that of the drafts of the thoroughbass exercises written in 1725–26. Its first movement was used in the Overture to *Scipione* (early 1726) and its third movement in the A major violin sonata (fair copy written on paper used between December 1725 and April 1726). It was therefore probably composed in 1725 or early 1726.

Second, the sixth and seventh movements of the D minor sonata were composed in draft on paper used between December 1725 and April 1726. The autograph of the whole sonata, written on paper used between December 1724 and early 1726, was presumably therefore made almost immediately afterwards. As stylistically the other movements of this sonata, especially the third and fifth, seem earlier than the last two movements and indeed the other five sonatas, perhaps Handel was drawing on material he had composed previously.[5]

Third, as we have shown (Critical Report, p. 70), the fair copies of the G minor, A minor, C major and F major sonatas, written on paper used between December 1725 and April 1726, contain a number of recomposed passages. The original versions of these sonatas, which form the basis of the S2 manuscript and the 'Roger' and Walsh prints, must have been written earlier. It need not have been very much earlier, however, since the original C minor violin version of the first movement of the A minor sonata is written on paper used between December 1724 and early 1726. Moreover, the second movement of the C major sonata, like the first movement of the Bb major sonata, was used for the Overture to *Scipione* (early 1726).[6] Thus these four sonatas could well have been composed in 1725–26 at the same time as the other two sonatas.

The 'Composition and Evaluation of the Sources' in our Critical Report is still valid in every respect but one.

Instead of '*c.* 1712' for the date of the autograph manuscripts, read 'probably 1725–26'. The chronology of the sources, their relationships to one another, and the weight given to each source in the preparation of the edition remain unchanged.

DAVID LASOCKI
Iowa City, Iowa, U.S.A.

WALTER BERGMANN
London, England

July 1982

1. We are extremely grateful to Mr Terence Best for sending us a detailed report of the results of this research and giving his own opinions on the dates of composition of the recorder sonatas. The researchers working on the study of paper-types are Mr Donald Burrows, Ms Martha Ronish and Mr Keiichiro Watanabe, to whom we are also most grateful for allowing us access to their preliminary findings.

2. Preface to Alfred Mann, ed., *Aufzeichnungen zur Kompositionslehre aus den Handschriften im Fitzwilliam Museum Cambridge/ Composition Lessons from the Autograph Collection in the Fitzwilliam Museum Cambridge*, Hallische Händel-Ausgabe, Supplement, Vol. 1 (Kassel: Bärenreiter, 1978), p. 80.

3. *Ibid.*, pp. 80–81.

4. *Ibid.*, p. 12.

5. We are most grateful to Mr Anthony Hicks for pointing this out to us.

6. The fifth movement of the flute sonata in E minor, Opus 1 No. 1a, to which we had assigned a composition date of *c.* 1720, is based on the fair-copy version of the fourth movement of the G minor recorder sonata. The recent paper studies, however, suggest a composition date of 1727–28 for the flute sonata, so that the chronology of the two uses of the movement in fact poses no problems.

Sonata No. 1 in G minor

Edited by
DAVID LASOCKI *and* WALTER BERGMANN

I

1) RW:

© 1979 by Faber Music Ltd

II

1) RW:

III

Adagio

6

Presto

IV

1) RSW:

1) RSW:

Sonata No. 2 in A minor

I

10

12

1) RSW:

III

Adagio

1) RSW: 2) RSW: 3) RSW:

14

1) RSW:

IV

Sonata No. 3 in C major

I

1) All sources: ♫

1) All sources: 2) RW: 3) All sources:

II

1) All sources:

III

IV

a Tempo di Gavotta

V

Sonata No. 4 in F major

I

1) ARSW:

II

1) ARSW: 2) RSW: 3) ARSW:

1) ARSW: 2) RSW: 3) ARSW:

IV

1) RSW:

40

1) ARSW:　　　　　　　2) ARSW:

Sonata No. 5 in B♭ major

I

II

1) Organ concerto:

III

Allegro

Sonata No. 6 in D minor

I

1) RW:

II

Vivace

1) AS:

III

IV

V

VI

VII

A tempo di menuet

APPENDIX

Early version of Sonata No. 2, fourth movement in C minor for violin

64

Early version of Sonata No. 6, sixth movement

Printed by Halstan & Co. Ltd., Amersham, Bucks., England

CRITICAL REPORT

Sources

Autograph Manuscripts

1. G minor sonata
   'Sonata a Flauto e Cembalo'
   Fitzwilliam Museum, Cambridge, MU. MS. 261, pp. 1–5.

2. A minor sonata
   a. 'Sonata a Flauto e Cembalo'
   British Library, R.M. 20. g. 13, ff. 12ᵛ–15ʳ.
   b. 'Sonata a Flauto e Cembalo'
   Fitzwilliam Museum, Cambridge, MU. MS. 163, p. 21
   (first two bars plus first two notes of recorder part of bar 3 only).

3. C major sonata
   Fitzwilliam Museum, Cambridge, MU. MS. 263, pp. 13–17
   (lacking first two pages – and therefore also a title – which contained the first movement and the first 66 bars of the second movement).

4. F major sonata
   'Sonata a Flauto e Cembalo'
   Fitzwilliam Museum, Cambridge, MU. MS. 261, pp. 7–11.

5. B♭ major sonata
   Fitzwilliam Museum, Cambridge, MU. MS. 260, pp. 13–15
   (lacking title).

6. D minor sonata
   a. Fitzwilliam Museum, Cambridge, MU. MS. 261, pp. 52–60 (lacking title).
   b. Fitzwilliam Museum, Cambridge, MU. MS. 263, p. 22 (alternative version of sixth movement only; lacking title).
   c. Fitzwilliam Museum, Cambridge, MU. MS. 263, p. 21 (alternative version of seventh movement only; found immediately after 2b above).

Copyists' Manuscripts

Five of the sonatas exist in a manuscript in the hand of the Handel copyist known as *S2*[1] in the Aylesford Collection[2] in the Henry Watson Music Library, Central Library, Manchester (press mark 130 Hd 4, Vol. 312):

1. G minor sonata
   'Sonata 3'
   pp. 11–14

2. A minor sonata
   'Sonata 5'
   pp. 20–6

3. C major sonata
   'Sonata 7'
   pp. 32–9

4. F major sonata
   'Sonata 6'
   pp. 27–31

6. D minor sonata
   'Sonata 8'
   pp. 40–9

Terence Best has pointed out that 'A feature of this manuscript is the copious addition of figures to the continuo in the hand of Charles Jennens, its first owner. These figures are sometimes correct indications of the harmony, but frequently are not.'[3] Jennens's figures can be distinguished from those of *S2* by the colour of the ink and, for the most part, by the writing.[4]

Three of the sonatas exist in a manuscript in a copyist's hand in a private collection in London (the owner of which has requested that he remain anonymous):

1. F major sonata
   'Sonata i a Flauto e Cembalo Dell Sigʳᵉ Hendel'

2. C major sonata
   'Sonata ii a Flauto e Cembalo'

3. D minor sonata
   'Sonata iii a Flauto e Cembalo'

It is perhaps significant that these sonatas appear here in the same order as in the *S2* manuscript (Sonatas 6–8).

Prints

1. 'SONATES / POUR UN / TRAVERSIERE / UN / VIOLON OU HAUTBOIS / Con Basso Continuo / Composées par / G. F. HANDEL / A AMSTERDAM / CHEZ JEANNE ROGER / N° 534' (actually published in London by John Walsh *c.* 1726–32 – see below).

2a. 'SOLOS / For a / GERMAN FLUTE / a HOBOY or VIOLIN / With a / Thorough Bass for the / HARPSICORD [*sic*] / or / BASS VIOLIN / Compos'd by / Mr. Handel. / Printed: and Sold by IOHN WALSH at the Harp and Hoboy in Catherine Street in the Strand. / . . . / Note: This is more Corect [*sic*] than the former Edition' (1732).[5]

2b. As 2a but with 'N° 407' added at the end of the title (*c.* 1733).[6]

3a. 'XII SOLOS / For a / GERMAN FLUTE / a HOBOY or VIOLIN / With a / Thorough Bass for the / HARPSICORD [*sic*] / or / BASS VIOLIN / Composé / Par Mʳ Handel / . . . / A Paris. Chez La Veuve Boivin . . . Le Sʳ Le Clerc . . . Le Sʳ Guersaut . . .' (*c.* 1737).[7]

3b. As 3a but with 'Le Sʳ Duval' instead of 'Le Sʳ Guersaut' (*c.* 1740).[8]

4. 'Twelve / SONATAS or SOLO'S / for the / GERMAN FLUTE, / HAUTBOY and VIOLIN. / Published about the Year 1724. / Composed by / G. F. HANDEL' (Arnold's Collected Edition, Vols. 139 and 140, *c.* 1793).[9]

The familiar modern designation of these collections as Opus 1 does not appear on any of the title pages, but was used by Walsh in advertisements from 1734 onwards.[10] Opus 1 contains five of the sonatas numbered and labelled (at the foot of the first page of each sonata) as follows:

1. G minor sonata. Opus 1 No. 2. 'Flauto Solo'.
2. A minor sonata. Opus 1 No. 4. 'Flauto Solo'.
3. C major sonata. Opus 1 No. 7. 'Flauto Solo'.
4. F major sonata. Opus 1 No. 11. 'Flauto Solo'.
5. D minor sonata (in B minor). Opus 1 No. 9. 'Traversa Solo'.

The other sonatas in the collection are No. 1 in E minor for flute (in D minor for violin in Handel's autograph), No. 3 in A major for violin, No. 5 in G major for flute (in F major in contemporary manuscripts, probably for oboe), No. 6 in G minor for oboe (for violin in the autograph), No. 8 in C minor for oboe, and Nos. 10 and 12 in A major and E major for violin (both of which are probably spurious).[11]

Walsh sold copies of the 'Roger' edition with his own label pasted over the imprint. Of this edition, Terence Best has written: 'Despite the Roger imprint, it is clear from the style of the engraving that the edition was prepared by John Walsh of London. Two other editions of Handel's instrumental music were published in the same way at this period – the *Pièces à un & Deux Clavecins* of c. 1719, and the trio sonatas Op. 2. . . . These editions were probably not authorised by the composer, which may explain why the Roger imprint was used.'[12] Until recently it has been assumed that, even though the 'Roger' edition was engraved by Walsh, it was still issued by Roger, as its title page claimed. New evidence suggests otherwise. Donald Burrows has examined the engraving style of the Handel Opus 1 and of a considerable number of the Walsh prints of the 1720s and '30s and concluded that the engraving of the Handel sonatas was done by two engravers (let us call them *A* and *B*). Following Burrows' lead, Terence Best has traced the earliest datable appearance of engraver *A* to a Walsh print of July 1724 (*The Monthly Mask of Vocal Musick*) and of engraver *B* to *Alexander for a Flute* in October 1726. These two engravers worked well into the 1730s, the bulk of their handiwork clustering around 1730.[13] Their engraving styles are distinguishable by the treble clefs and by the notation for a trill (*A* writes *tr*, *B* writes *t*). Engraver *B* was responsible for three of the four recorder sonatas (A minor, C major and F major) and the G major flute sonata; engraver *A* did the remainder. Now, Jeanne Roger died in 1722. Clearly, if the style of the engraving did not appear until at least 1726, she could not have published the Handel Opus 1.

Another piece of evidence Best discovered is that the water-mark on the title page of one of the British Library copies of the 1732 Walsh edition (pressmark g. 74. c) is identical to that on the title page of the British Library copy of the 'Roger' edition (pressmark g. 74. d). While it is not completely out of the question that Jeanne Roger in Amsterdam could have been using the same paper in 1722 or earlier as Walsh in London in 1732 (some paper used in England was made in the Netherlands), it seems improbable.

A close comparison between the 'Roger' title page and some genuine Jeanne Roger title pages reveals that the lettering and layout on the 'Roger' title page are a fairly good imitation of her style, but they are not the same. Furthermore, the plate number is erroneous. Estienne Roger's editions were published until the year 1716 without any plate numbers on the title pages. In that year, before he died and passed his business on to his daughter Jeanne, he (or she) gave plate numbers to all his left-over stock in an arbitrary manner. But from 1716 onwards all editions of Estienne Roger, Jeanne Roger (1716–22) and Estienne's son-in-law Michel-Charles Le Cène (1723–43) were given plate numbers in chronological order, making it possible to date them accurately by this means. Now, Jeanne Roger's editions covered plate numbers 420–95. The plate number 534 of the Handel Opus 1 'Roger' edition would correspond to a Le Cène edition of 1727 and did in fact belong to the second volume of Vivaldi's Opus 9 published at that time.[14] In other words, the 'Roger' title page is a fake.

If more evidence were needed, one may also take into consideration the distribution among modern libraries of copies of the 'Roger' and Walsh prints. The Walsh edition of 1732 is found in one British and one Continental library. The Walsh edition of c. 1733 is found in two British and six Continental libraries. Yet, significantly, the 'Roger' print, ostensibly published on the Continent not in England, is found in only two Continental but five British libraries.

All this evidence suggests very strongly that Walsh was completely responsible for the production of the 'Roger' edition and that it was issued somewhere between 1726 and 1732.[15] The question remains, why did he go to the trouble of faking the Roger title page and selling copies of the edition with his own label pasted over the false imprint? The explanation offered by Best, that the edition was not authorised by Handel, still seems the most plausible.

In the light of what we know of the relations between Handel and Walsh at this period,[16] the circumstances of publication were probably as follows. Around 1730, Walsh obtained copies of ten sonatas by Handel without the 'Consent or Approbation' of the composer. He wanted to publish works for the newly-popular transverse flute as well as the ever-popular violin and (to a lesser extent) the oboe.[17] Five of the sonatas he had obtained were for the recorder (four, as we shall see, in early drafts which antedate the autograph fair copies of c. 1712) but because of the keys and range could be played on the flute or violin as they stood. He left four of them alone but transposed the D minor sonata into B minor for the flute. (Alternatively, but less likely in view of the fact that all three extant manuscripts are in D minor, Handel may already have transposed the sonata himself.) Three of the sonatas were for the violin (in D minor, A major and G minor). He transposed the first into E minor for the flute,[18] left the second alone, and labelled the third for the oboe. The remaining two sonatas were for the oboe (in F major and C minor). He transposed the first into G major for the flute and left the second alone. Presumably to round out the customary set of twelve sonatas, he added two violin sonatas by another composer in what he thought would pass for Handel's style. Since he wanted to improve his relations with the composer, or to continue newly-won good relations, he was reluctant to assume full responsibility for perpetrating this motley collection and wondered how he could shift some of the blame elsewhere. He remembered the arrangement he had had with Jeanne Roger around 1719 whereby he engraved the music of Handel's harpsichord pieces and she issued the edition with her own title page, and he must have known that she had died in 1722. Since she was no longer around to protest, what better than to pretend that she had published this new edition but then to put his own label over the imprint and sell the sonatas himself as if he had merely imported them from Amsterdam (forbidden by Handel's royal privilege of 1720 but more defensible)? He therefore drew up a title page in Jeanne Roger's style – and since he was primarily interested in the flute, violin and oboe market he did not mention that four of the sonatas were for the recorder but relegated the instrumentation to the bottom of the first page of each sonata – invented a plate number, and had the sonatas engraved by his current engravers. (He adopted the same plan for the trio sonatas, Opus 2.)[19] Later, having established good relations with Handel for a while, he could own up to the edition and engraved a new Walsh title page and took the opportunity to correct some of the mistakes of the earlier edition (see below). Handel had by then presumably given up hope of monitoring Walsh's activities and did not bother to insist that the remaining mistakes be corrected.[20]

The corrections vaunted on the title page of the Walsh edition of 1732 were both major and minor. In the recorder sonatas the major alterations were the restoration of the fourth movement of the C major sonata (previously omitted) and of the sixth movement of the B minor flute version of the D minor sonata (previously printed as the third movement of the G major flute sonata). A handful of minor changes were made in the bass figures, slurs, rhythms, notes and tempo markings. All the newly-engraved material was done by engraver *A*.

The other editions listed above are unimportant for our purposes. The two French editions are based on the 1732 Walsh edition, and the Arnold edition on 'Roger'.

Instrumentation

The autograph manuscripts of the G minor, A minor and F major sonatas are all marked 'Sonata a Flauto e Cembalo', and there can be no doubt that they were intended for the treble recorder and basso continuo. At the beginning of the eighteenth century, the plain word 'flute' (*flauto* in Italian; *flûte* in French) referred to the recorder, not the transverse flute, which received a qualifying adjective meaning either transverse or German. (Handel designates the flute by the word 'Traversa' in the autograph of the E minor sonata known as Opus 1 No. 1a.)[21] The presence of the bass figures indicates basso continuo (a keyboard instrument with or without a bass instrument such as a violoncello or viola da gamba).

Since these three sonatas plus the C major sonata are labelled 'Flauto Solo' in the prints, and since the C major sonata is headed 'Sonata a Flauto Solo e Cembalo' in the manuscript in the private collection in London, it is reasonable to suppose that the missing title page of this sonata in the autograph manuscript would also have been headed thus (or in some other way that

would have shown conclusively that it was intended for the treble recorder).

The B♭ major sonata has no indication of instrumentation; but the attribution to the recorder, first made by Thurston Dart,[22] makes sense on the evidence of the key, range (f′ to e♭′′′) and concordances. When Handel used the third movement again in his A major violin sonata, he changed the key to A major, which would seem to eliminate the possibility that the B♭ major version is for the violin. The other possibilities are the flute and the oboe. The key would be suitable for the oboe, but less so for the flute. The range is too high for the oboe; and all Handel's genuine flute and oboe sonatas go significantly below f′ (the flute sonata to d′, the oboe sonatas to c′ or d′).

The D minor sonata also has no indication of instrumentation in the autograph manuscript. But Dart's attribution to the recorder is again warranted by the key, range (f′ to d′′′), concordances and heading 'Sonata a Flauto e Cembalo' in the manuscript in the private collection in London. The relationship of a minor third between the keys of this version and the flute version in B minor is customary for recorder music at this period. Furthermore, the early autograph version of the sonata's sixth movement is found on a page that begins with the heading 'Sonata a Flauto e Cembalo' (and the first two bars and two notes of the A minor recorder sonata).

A Comparison and Evaluation of the Sources

As we have seen, Handel's six recorder sonatas are extant in four different classes of sources. First, the autograph manuscripts of all six sonatas. Second, the manuscripts of five of them in the hand of the reliable Handel copyist known as *S2*. Third, the manuscripts of three of them in the hand of another copyist. And fourth, the 'Roger' and Walsh prints, again of five of the sonatas but with the D minor sonata transposed to B minor for the flute.

The autographs of the G minor, A minor, C major and F major sonatas are fair copies, written in a large, bold, neat hand with practically no corrections. Handel used this style of writing around 1712 (e.g. in *Rinaldo*) and also for fair copies up to about 1720, although he usually used a copyist for such a task from 1717 onwards. The paper suggests a dating of *c*. 1712.[23] The autographs of the B♭ major and D minor sonatas, on the other hand, are written much more sloppily, and the D minor sonata in particular contains many corrections. They are written on some Italian paper, which Handel must have obtained during his travels in Italy from the end of 1706 to the end of 1709. This does not necessarily mean that they were composed in Italy, for works as late as the keyboard sketch for the overture to *Amadigi* (1715) were written on the same paper. Best dates them *c*. 1712 again, on the grounds of the writing style and the surrounding pieces in this section of the manuscript.[24]

Best has noted that the *S2* manuscript was written 'in the early 1730s, and may have been copied before the issue of the Walsh edition of 1732. . . . In some of the sonatas there are differences of detail between the autographs and the Roger and Walsh texts; the [*S2*] copy sometimes has the autograph readings and sometimes those of Roger, to which it is nearer than to Walsh. This suggests that it was copied, not from the autographs, but from another manuscript related to that which was used in the preparation of the edition, a manuscript which may have incorporated late corrections by Handel.'[25]

The manuscript in the private collection in London shows no clear correspondence with any of the other sources. The F major sonata is very close to the prints and *S2*; the C major sonata has more features of the autograph than of the prints or *S2*; and the D minor sonata leans more to the prints and *S2* but has some significant details of the autograph.

The first print of the sonatas, the 'Roger' edition, was published *c*. 1726–32, almost two decades after Handel made his fair copies of the G minor, A minor, C major and F major sonatas. Nevertheless, some details in the prints and *S2* manuscript of these four sonatas show that they must have been based on earlier versions of the music. First, the fourth movement of the G minor sonata begins in the prints and *S2* manuscript as shown in Fig. 1, line 2. The autograph, on the other hand, has the reading given in line 1. When Handel reworked the movement in later compositions (see Concordances below), he moved the bar-line so that the movement begins on the half-bar, but otherwise followed the autograph of the recorder sonata rather than the prints or *S2* (see line 3).

Fig. 1

Second, Handel reworked the entire F major sonata into an organ concerto around 1735.[26] In six significant instances, the prints and *S2* have different readings from the autograph (five of them are shown in Fig. 2) but the organ concerto follows the autograph. That the autograph is not only different from but later than the prints and *S2* is suggested in one instance on musical grounds: the slides in the autograph at m. 14 of the fourth movement are an ornamented version of the reading of the prints and *S2*.

Fig. 2

Throughout these four sonatas, in addition to the cases just mentioned, the sources differ on details of bass figures (not always amounting to an intended change of the harmony), rhythms, ornaments, articulations, tempo markings, time signatures, and even notes. As Best has remarked, *S2* sometimes follows the autograph and sometimes the 'Roger' or Walsh print; occasionally it has still another reading. On the whole the autographs are better endowed with articulation marks and appoggiaturas than the prints. But the prints tend to be marked with more trills (cadential and passing), which are the only other ornaments indicated. Handel could easily have marked these trills in his first version and neglected to write them in when he made the fair copies (in any case, he almost never indicated obvious cadential trills). In making the fair copies he also made changes in rhythm for a number of note-values smaller than the pulses,[27] which is probably evidence of the freedom the performer was given at that time to play such note-values with whatever degree of inequality of length he wished.

To sum up, the chronology of the sources of the G minor, A minor, C major and F major sonatas seems to have been as follows. First, Handel composed the original version (*Q1*) around 1712. At about the same time he made a fair copy of the sonatas (*M*) and in the process recomposed a number of passages. Around 1730, Walsh engraved the sonatas without the authorisation of the composer, either from *Q1* itself or a source very like it (*Q2*), but making both major and minor mistakes, either from carelessness or because they occurred in the source used. In the early 1730s, probably by 1732, *S2* copied the sonatas, apparently from still another source (*Q3*), which incorporated some but not all of the changes Handel made for *M*. Finally, in 1732, Walsh printed a corrected version of the sonatas, either from the same source as previously but more carefully, or from a different source (*Q1* or *Q2*, or still another source, *Q4*).

For the B♮ major sonata there is only one source – the autograph manuscript. As mentioned above, this is not a fair copy but rather a first draft, upon which a number of minor corrections are visible. If Handel ever made a fair copy of this sonata, it is not extant. For this reason the autograph does not represent Handel's final thoughts on the work in the same way that the autographs of the G minor, A minor, C major and F major sonatas do. The fact that he borrowed all three movements for use in later pieces is therefore of the greatest significance, especially the use of the third movement in the violin sonata in A major, Opus 1 No. 3, which was written very soon after the recorder sonata, and the concordances are helpful for clearing up some puzzling passages in the original version.

The D minor sonata presents the most complex problems in establishing the chronology of the sources and the definitive text. The sources are: an autograph manuscript (*M**) in D minor of the sixth and seventh movements only; the autograph manuscript (*M*) in D minor of the complete sonata, which, like that of the B♭ major sonata, contains corrections; a manuscript in D minor in the hand of *S2* (*S*); a manuscript in D minor in the private collection in London (*O*); and the 'Roger' (*R*) and Walsh (*W*) prints, transposed into B minor for the transverse flute.

As we have seen, *M* dates from *c.* 1712. *M** is written on the same paper that Handel used in his early English period as the fair copies of the G minor, A minor, C major and F major sonatas and thus dates from around the same time.[28] On musical grounds, *M** seems to be the earliest source of all. Its version of the 6/8 seventh movement was written first in 3/8; the time signature still reads 3/8, although every second bar-line has been crossed out. All the other sources have this movement in 6/8. The *M** version of the sixth movement opens with a figure (also occurring five times in the second half) that is omitted completely from the other versions. There are many repetitions of the figure marked A in Fig. 3, and the episode at mm. 14–22 again utilises this figure (see Fig. 4a). In writing *M*, Handel changed one occurrence of figure A near the beginning of the movement (m. 5) (see Fig. 3, line 2) and replaced the above-mentioned episode with a much shorter and (in our opinion) more effective one based on a chromatic scale (Fig. 4b). He then crossed out all the figures in mm. 2–5, substituting for two of them figure B, which is a partly ornamented and partly de-ornamented version of figure A (Fig. 3, line 3). The movement as found in *S*, *O*, *R* and *W* seems to represent the final stage in the process of composition. At the beginning of the movement Handel reinstated figure A but retained figure B, producing the order BABA, which to our mind is also the most satisfying (Fig. 3, line 4).

Fig. 3

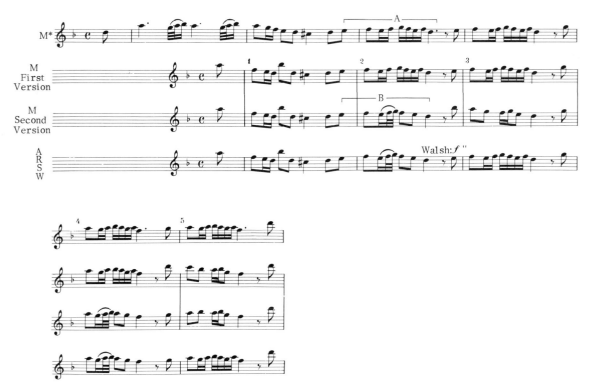

Fig. 4

Apart from demonstrating Handel's compositional skill with somewhat unpromising material, this detective work on the sixth movement suggests that the autograph manuscripts present only his first thoughts on the sonata. This is confirmed by a study of other details in the sonata. *S*, *O* and especially *R* and *W* have better bass figures than *M*; they also have more articulation marks and fewer trills than the autograph, the reverse of the situation with the prints and fair copies of the first four sonatas (see above).

R and *W* have identical texts for all the movements except the sixth. This movement was omitted from the sonata in *R* and placed instead in the G major flute sonata. For *W*, therefore, a new plate had to be engraved. In the process some changes crept in: the omission of a slur; the alteration of five notes, five bass figures and one rhythm; and the omission of five bass figures. In all cases except one passage in which three notes are brought down an octave in *W* (also found in *S*), *R* seems to have the better text. Throughout the sonata, apart from minor details *S* is close to *R*.

To sum up, the chronology of the sources of the D minor sonata seems to be as follows. First, Handel composed versions of the sixth and seventh movements (*M**) around 1712. Soon afterwards he composed the whole sonata (*M*), making a number of alterations in the sixth and seventh movements. Around 1730, Walsh engraved the sonata without the authorisation of the composer, not from *M* or *M** but from a source not extant (*P1*) which incorporated further alterations by the composer and may have omitted the sixth movement; the transposition to B minor for the flute may also have been found in *P1* or may have been made by Walsh. In the early 1730s, probably by 1732, *S2* copied the sonata (*S*), either from *P1* (if that was in D minor) or a similar source *P2* (if *P1* was in B minor and/or omitted the sixth movement). Finally, in 1732, Walsh printed an allegedly corrected version of the sonata, restoring the sixth movement but making a number of mistakes in re-engraving the plate; his source was either *P1* (if that had the sixth movement) or an otherwise identical source (*P2* or *P3*) that had the sixth movement (if *P1* did not).

Establishing a Text

In preparing this edition, we have worked on the principle that the text should present Handel's final thoughts on these sonatas. Our primary sources have therefore been: for the G minor, A minor, C major (except for the first movement and first 66 bars of the second movement) and F major sonatas – the autograph manuscript; for the beginning of the C major sonata – the *S2* manuscript and the Walsh print; for the B♮ major sonata – the autograph manuscript modified by the evidence of the concordances; and for the D minor sonata – the *S2* manuscript and 'Roger' print.

The variant readings found in the secondary sources have been dealt with in two ways. First, the most significant readings from secondary or alternative primary sources are given at the bottom of the page in question. Second, all the differences among the sources (except for bass figures where an alternative reading does not signify a change in the harmony itself) are listed together below under 'Differences Among the Sources'.

Concordances

G minor sonata

Second movement = second movement of flute sonata in E minor known as Opus 1 No. 1a (*c.* 1720; autograph in British Library, R. M. 20.g.13, ff. 9^r–11^r).

Fourth movement = fifth movement of flute sonata in E minor, Opus 1 No. 1a.

Also = fourth movement of organ concerto in G minor, Opus 4 No. 3 (written *c.* 1735–6, published 1738) (with divisions).

Also = fourth movement of organ concerto in G minor, Opus 7 No. 5 (*c.* 1750) (different ending).

A minor sonata

First movement. Bass similar to that of 'Se non giunge' in solo cantata *Filli adorata* (*c.* 1707–9) (HG Vol. 50, p. 90) and also to that of 'Pur ritorno a rimirarvi' from *Agrippina* (1709) (HG Vol 57, p. 47).

Fourth movement. Early version in C minor for violin and basso continuo (*c.* 1711; autograph in Fitzwilliam Museum, Cambridge, MU. MS. 260, pp. 19–20): see Appendix to the sonata in the present edition.

C major sonata

Second movement = first *allegro* in Overture to *Scipione* (1726).

Third movement = third movement of flute sonata in G major, Opus 1 No. 5 (originally in F major, probably for oboe; copy in hand of *S2* in Manchester Central Library, 130 Hd 4, Vol. 312, pp. 50–4).
Bass similar to that of aria 'Tears are my daily food' in fourth version of sixth Chandos Anthem, *As Pants the Hart* (*c.* 1716–20) (HG Vol 36, p. 237).

F major sonata

Complete as organ concerto in F major, Opus 4 No. 5 (probably first performed 1735, published 1738).

B♮ major sonata

First movement = second *allegro* in Overture to *Scipione* (1726).

Second movement = third movement of organ concerto in F major, Opus 4 No. 4 (written 1735, published 1738).

Third movement = third movement of violin sonata in A major, Opus 1 No. 3 (*c.* 1712; autograph in Fitzwilliam Museum, Cambridge, MU. MS. 261, pp. 13–19).

D minor sonata

Fifth movement = fugue in third of *Twelve Voluntaries and Fugues for the Organ or Harpsicord . . . Book IV* (London: Longman & Broderip, *c.* 1780 or later) and first of *6 Fugues faciles pour l'orgue ou Piano Forte* (Vienna: Traeg, *c.* 1803; Cappi & Diabelli, *c.* 1818–24; Diabelli, 1824 or later) (HG Vol. 48, p. 183).

Seventh movement found twice in a collection of minuets (with no indication of instrumentation, but possibly intended for keyboard) in an Aylesford manuscript in the hand of Smith junior (British Library, R. M. 18.b.8, ff. 74^v and 79^r).

Doubtful Attributions

In 1948, Thurston Dart published an edition of three 'Fitzwilliam Sonatas', as he called them, for treble recorder and basso continuo.[29] The reason for the name was of course that he discovered the manuscripts of these sonatas in the Fitzwilliam Museum, Cambridge. The first sonata in this collection was the B♮ recorder sonata that forms part of the present edition. The third sonata was the D minor recorder sonata, but shorn of the last two of its seven movements. Dart gave no more details, but elsewhere he claimed that 'The Fitzwilliam autograph of [the B minor flute sonata] (transposed up a third for recorder, which may well have been the work's original form) omits the last two movements of what is already an immensely long sonata.'[30] One wonders why Dart failed to see that these two movements were in fact present in the manuscript. The second sonata was also in D minor and, it was claimed, had been 'assembled by the editor from widely scattered copies of its movements' in three of the Fitzwilliam Handel volumes. This so-called sonata was actually the early versions of the seventh and sixth movements (in that order) of the real D minor sonata, coupled with a minuet found, without indication of instrumentation, in another volume of the manuscripts, and which Dart changed from 6/8 time to 3/4 time.

In 1974, Klaus Hofmann published an edition of three Handel recorder sonatas, which were again called 'Fitzwilliam-Sonaten'.[31] The first and second were the B♭ major and D minor sonatas, the latter in its full seven-movement form (and with the early and flute-sonata versions of its sixth movement given in appendices). The third sonata, in G major, had never previously been attributed to the recorder. Fuller-Maitland and Mann, in their catalogue of the Fitzwilliam Museum collection, had ascribed it to the harpsichord, which, as Hofmann rightly points out, cannot be true, because there are bass figures in the second movement. Hofmann believed it to be in fact for treble recorder, on two grounds: 1. the lowest note of the piece is g', whereas all Handel's sonatas for flute, oboe and violin go below this note (and indeed below f'); 2. a passage at the end of the first movement makes a 'surprising' move up to g'' instead of going down to g', in order, so he believed, to avoid the low $f\sharp'$ which would have been difficult to play on the recorders of the time. He concedes that the sonata would make far greater technical demands on the performer than Handel's other recorder sonatas – the writing is higher (e''' is common), and the first movement consists of an unbroken chain of semiquavers, causing breathing problems for a recorder player – but is still not deterred from making the attribution to the recorder. What he cannot explain satisfactorily is a genuinely surprising passage in the third movement where the melody instrument has the notes b''' c'''' d''' e''''. He suggests that Handel really meant to write a''' b''' c'''' d'''' or e''' $f\sharp'''$ g''' d''', ignoring the fact that Handel deliberately changed clef to accommodate this unusually high passage; besides, Hofmann's suggested alternatives are still unplayable or unthinkable on the treble recorder of the day.[32] The only melody instrument of the time that was capable of performing this very high passage is the violin, which could also have coped easily with the technical demands of the first movement, and the sonata is ascribed to the violin by Best in his recent study of the Handel sonatas.[33]

Footnotes

1. On Handel's copyists in general and *S2* in particular, see Jens Peter Larsen, *Handel's Messiah: Origins, Compositions, Sources* (Adam & Charles Black, London, 1957), pp. 260–1, 264, 267, facsimiles on pp. 310, 314.

2. Winton Dean has written of the Aylesford manuscripts: 'The bulk of the manuscripts originally belonged to Handel's friend Charles Jennens, librettist of *Saul, L'Allegro, Messiah* and *Belshazzar,* at whose order they were supplied by the group of copyists working under Handel's principal amanuensis, John Christopher Smith the elder. At Jennens' death in 1773 they passed by inheritance to his cousin the third Earl of Aylesford (1715–77), also a friend of Handel.' See his foreword to *George Frideric Handel: The Newman Flower Collection in the Henry Watson Music Library: A Catalogue,* compiled by Arthur D. Walker (The Manchester Public Libraries, 1972).

3. Terence Best, 'Handel's Solo Sonatas', *Music & Letters* LVIII/4 (October 1977), pp. 430–8; 434.

4. See the facsimile of Jennens's writing in Larsen, op. cit., p. 323.

5. It was advertised on *The Most Celebrated Songs in the Oratorio call'd Queen Esther to which is prefixt the Overture in Score Compos'd by Mr. Handel . . . London . . . Walsh . . . N.° 288:* 'The following Musick Compos'd by Mr. Handel, which may be had, where these are Sold. . . . Twelve Solos for a Violin or German Flute, with a Thorough Bass for the Harpsicord. . . .' *Esther* itself was advertised in the *Daily Journal,* 25 November 1732; see William C. Smith, *Handel, A Descriptive Catalogue of the Early Editions,* 2nd edn. (Basil Blackwell, Oxford, 1970), pp. 104, 243.

6. Dating from Smith, ibid., p. 243.

7. Dating from ibid. See also Cecil Hopkinson, 'Handel and France: Editions Published there during his Lifetime', *Edinburgh Bibliographical Society Transactions* III/4 (1957).

8. Dating from Smith, op. cit., p. 244.

9. Dating from Best, op. cit., p. 432.

10. The advertisement in *The Country Journal; or, The Craftsman,* 7 December 1734, reads: '. . . Twelve Solo's for a Violin, German Flute or Harpsicord. Opera Prima.'

11. For full details see Best, op. cit.

12. Ibid., p. 431.

13. Terence Best, telephone conversations with David Lasocki, 2 August and 27 September 1978.

14. See François Lesure, *Bibliographie des éditions musicales publiées par Estienne Roger et Michel-Charles Le Cène (Amsterdam, 1696–1743),* Publications de la Société Française de Musicologie, Deuxième série, Tome XII (Société Française de Musicologie/Heugel, Paris, 1969), pp. 10, 23, [91] and the Le Cène catalogue of *c.* 1737 found at the end of this book, p. 62.

15. That Walsh chose to fake a Jeanne Roger plate number equivalent to one of her successor's dating from around 1727 is perhaps evidence that the 'Roger' edition dates from closer to 1727 than to 1732. On the other hand, the label that Walsh stuck over the false Roger imprint seems to date from between 14 February and 25 November 1732. (The list of Handel's compositions found on the label includes all those in Walsh's first collective advertisement of his Handel publications of 14 February 1732 and three more in addition, one of which, 'Tunes in the Alchimist', was apparently not published until later in the year since it was first advertised on *Esther,* itself advertised on 25 November 1732. The list on the title page of the Walsh edition of the Opus 1 sonatas is identical to that on the label from the 'Roger' edition, except that the price of 'Apollo's Feast' has been increased from £3. 1s. 0d. to £3. 3s. 0d, suggesting that the label was slightly earlier.) If the labels and

'Roger' editions were printed at the same time—which may or may not have been the case—this evidence suggests a publication date much closer to that of the Walsh edition itself. Since none of the evidence is conclusive, we have kept to the range of dates *c*. 1726–32 for the present.

16. On 14 June 1720, King George I granted Handel a privilege of copyright to protect him against pirated publications. It gave him licence 'for the sole Printing and Publishing' of his works for fourteen years, and it forbade anyone to 'Reprint or Abridge' them 'or to Import, Buy, Vend, Utter or Distribute any Copies thereof Reprinted beyond the Seas, during the said Term of Fourteen Years, without the Consent or Approbation of the said George Frederick Handel, his Heirs, Executors and Assigns. . . .' Handel may have sought this remedy because around 1720 Jeanne Roger in Amsterdam issued an edition of some of his keyboard suites that had not previously been published. (See the Le Cène catalogue of 1737 found in Lesure, op. cit., p. 69: '490. Suites de Piéces pour le Clavessin composée par G. F. Hendel'. The plate number confirms the dating of 1720 implied by Handel's denunciation. That Roger did publish the edition is supported by the fact that her successor, Le Cène, later reissued it with his own imprint, a copy of which is now in the Hoboken collection.) As mentioned above, the engraving of the music was actually done by Walsh in London. (It is in the Walsh engraving style of *c*. 1719–20. Best, telephone conversation with David Lasocki, 27 September 1978.) This publication was unauthorised by Handel, who replied by issuing some of the suites himself, engraved and printed by John Cluer 'for the Author', and advertising: 'Note, The Author has been obliged to publish these Pieces to prevent the Publick being imposed upon by some Surreptitious and incorrect Copies of some of them that has got abroad'. (Advertisement in the *Daily Courant*, 9 November 1720.) Walsh sold this official edition with his label pasted over the imprint. (See Smith, op. cit., p. 248.)

In the early 1720s, most of Handel's operatic productions with the Royal Academy of Music were engraved and printed by Cluer. Yet the trick of engraving the harpsichord suites but having Roger put her name to the edition must have averted suspicion from Walsh enough for him to establish good relations with Handel, for Walsh too issued some of these operas as 'Publish'd by the Author' with Handel's privilege, until the *Flavio* of 1723. But even by this date relations between Handel and Walsh may have soured. In 1722 Walsh put out a pirated arrangement for recorder of *Radamisto*, and 'The favourite Songs in the Opera call'd Acis and Galatea' (which Handel had not released for publication) without the composer's name. (Ibid., pp. 54, 81.) There are no entries in the (admittedly sketchy) Walsh Cash-Book from 1723 to 1729, and from 1724 to his death in 1730 Cluer was 'in some way the official publisher for the Academy productions'. (Ibid., p. xiv.) On the other hand, in the mid 1720s Walsh started to issue his large collections of pieces from Handel operas which continued until after the composer's death (*Overtures*, 1723 etc.; *Sonatas or Chamber Aires*, *c*. 1725; *Apollo's Feast*, 1726 etc.), and William C. Smith has remarked that 'It can hardly be assumed that Handel was quite disinterested in these Walsh productions and had no financial interest in them'. (Ibid., p. xv.) Nevertheless, after Walsh had issued 'Favourite Songs' from *Tamerlano* in 1724 ('Printed and Sold at the Musick Shops' and without an imprint) almost as soon as Cluer had the vocal score ready, the authorised edition of the recorder arrangements was prefaced with a note declaring pointedly that 'If J. Cluer's Name is not in the Title Pages of those Works, they are spurious [*sic*] Editions, and not those Corrected and Figur'd by Mr. Handel'.

From May 1725 onwards, 'Handel did not use his privilege of 1720 any more, probably being aware of its worthlessness against Walsh and his consorts' (other publishing pirates). (Otto Deutsch, *Handel, A Documentary Biography*, Adam & Charles Black, London, 1955, p. 180.) Finally, from *Parthenope*, advertised on 4 April 1730, 'Walsh settled down as Handel's regular publisher' and 'the Walshes, father and son, had an unbroken business association with Handel until his death'. (Smith, loc. cit.) As Deutsch has pointed out, 'the prohibition of reprints' granted in the privilege 'was not always observed and the fact that Walsh was the most successful of the London music pirates seems to have been the reason why Handel finally went over to Walsh's camp for good'. (Deutsch, op. cit., p. 106.)

17. Although the oboe is mentioned on the title pages of both 'Roger' and Walsh editions, Walsh always advertised the collection as being for flute, or for flute or violin.

18. He may have been aware that Handel himself had transposed the first and fourth movements of this sonata into E minor for flute as part of the sonata now known as Opus 1 No. 1a (autograph, British Library, R.M. 20. g. 13, ff. 9–11). See Best, 'Handel's Solo Sonatas', p. 433.

19. He faked a title page as follows: 'VI SONATES / à deux Violons, deux haubois ou / deux Flutes traversieres & / Basse Continue / Composées Par / G. F. HANDEL / SECOND OUVRAGE / A AMSTERDAM / CHEZ JEANNE ROGER / N° 535'. When he came to make up his own title page later, he did not even bother to fashion a new one but simply left the top half of the page intact and re-engraved the imprint: '. . . Walsh . . . Note. This is more Corect [*sic*] than the former Edition. N°. 408'. The Walsh label on the 'Roger' Opus 2 is identical to that on the 'Roger' Opus 1.

20. Corrections to published editions by the composer may not have been common at this time. Richard Meares, for example, advertising the official edition of *Radamisto* in the *Post-Boy*, 12 July 1720, boasted that 'To make this Work the more acceptable, the Author has been prevailed with to correct the whole'. That Walsh could still leave mistakes in officially-sanctioned publications of Handel's is shown by his edition of the second volume of the keyboard suites, which is full of curious errors, some of them left over from the pieces included in the Roger/Walsh edition of *c*. 1720. (Best, telephone conversation with David Lasocki, 27 September 1978.)

21. See footnote 17.

22. For his edition of the sonata (Schott, London, 1948).

23. This was pointed out to us by Terence Best (telephone conversation with David Lasocki, 30 May 1978).

24. Letter to David Lasocki, 20 June 1978.

25. Best, 'Handel's Solo Sonatas', pp. 433–4.

26. 'To compose the concerto, Handel had his copyist write out the recorder sonata in F, Op. 1 no. 11, and simply added supporting orchestral parts round it, sometimes filling out the recorder line with simple additional harmony. The first movement, a *larghetto*, is unchanged in outline; the orchestra parts happily add an occasional imitation, perhaps suggesting what Handel visualised a continuo player's doing. In the *allegro* second movement he added a five-bar orchestra ritornello at the start, the same music as the first five bars of solo; otherwise he used the orchestra merely to reinforce the final cadence of each half. In the brief *siciliana* he added a two-bar orchestral introduction and filled out the texture; for the gigue-style finale (altered from *allegro* to *presto*) he again added two bars at the beginning and a further two to round off each half. Few concertos can have been as painlessly composed'. Stanley Sadie, *Handel Concertos*, BBC Music Guides (BBC Publications, London, 1972), p. 29.

27. The pulse notes are generally quavers in C, ₵, 3/8, 6/8 and 12/8, crotchets in 3/4 and minims in 3/2, to mentioned only the time signatures used by Handel in these sonatas.
28. This was pointed out to us by Terence Best (telephone conversation with David Lasocki, 22 June 1978).
29. Schott, London (Edition Schott 10062).
30. In his review of the Hallische Händel-Ausgabe edition of the Opus I flute and recorder sonatas in *Music & Letters* XXXVII (1956), p. 402.
31. Neuhausen-Stuttgart: Hänssler, 1974 (HE 11.222, 11.223, 11.224).
32. The English recorders of the period tended to be weak in the high register; this is presumably why Handel avoids e′′′ and f′′′ in these sonatas (except for one instance in the A minor sonata—fourth movement, m.44). Continental recorders generally had a stronger high register, and some late fingering charts (Germany, 1732; England, *c.* 1750; Spain, 1754; Holland, 1795) went up to a′′′, b′′′ or even c′′′′, although never to the d′′′′ and e′′′′ found in this G major sonata. See David Lasocki, '17th and 18th Century Fingering Charts for the Recorder', *American Recorder* XI/4 (Fall, 1970), pp. 128–35; 134–5. That a recorder sonata going up to even a′′′ would be written in Italy *c.* 1707 (dating from Best, 'Handel's Solo Sonatas', p. 437) seems unlikely.
33. Ibid.

Differences Among the Sources

The following list contains all the differences among the sources of articulations, notes, ornaments, rhythms, tempos and time signatures. It includes bass figures only where these are both correct and apparently signify an intentionally different harmony.

Abbreviations:

A   Copyist's manuscript in private collection in London
M   Autograph manuscript
M2 Autograph manuscript of early version of 7th movement of D minor sonata
R   'Roger' print
S   Manuscript in hand of the copyist *S2*
W   Walsh print
app   appoggiatura
bc   basso continuo
fig   bass figure(s)
m   measure(s)/bar(s)
n   note(s)
rec   recorder

G minor Sonata

First movement

m1	rec	n2–3	no slur	RW
		n5–6	no slur	MRW
m2	rec	n4–5	[♩. ♪ tr]	RW
m4	rec	n1–2	no slur	RW
		n4–5	no slur	RSW
m5	rec	n1–2	no slur	RW
		n3–4	no slur	RW
m7	bc	n2–3	[notation]	RW
		n7	[notation]	RW; ♯ S
m12	bc	n1	no fig	RSW
m14	rec	n5	tr	S
m18	rec	n1–3	no slur	RSW

		n7–8	[♩. ♪]	RW
m19	rec	n2–3	slur	RW
		n2	tr	S

Second movement

m2	rec	n1	tr	S
m6	rec	n3–5	[notation] without slur	RW
		n6–8	no slur	RSW
m7	rec	n2	no stroke	RW
m8	rec	n3–4	no strokes	S
		n6–7	no strokes	S
m9	rec	n2	no stroke	RW
	bc	n1	no fig	RW
m10	rec	n3–5	slur	S; no slur RW
		n6–8	slur	S; no slur RW
m11	rec	n2	no stroke	MRW
m12	rec	n3–5	slur over 3 notes	RSW

and continuing throughout the movement

m13	rec	n2	no stroke	MRW
m23	bc	n1–2	no fig	RW
m24	rec	n3	tr	S
m27	bc	n1–2	no fig	RW
m28	rec	n3–4	[notation]	S
m29	rec	n1–2	no slur	RW
		n1–3	slur	S
			no app	RSW
m30	bc	n1	no fig	RSW
m39	rec	n2	a′′♭	RW
	bc	n1	6/5♭	RW
m41	rec	n2–3	slur	RW
		n4–6	slur	RW
m42	rec	n1–2	slur	S
m47	rec	n1–2	[notation]	S
	bc	n2	6	RW
m53	bc	n1–2	no fig	RW
m54	rec	n3–4	[notation]	RW
m55	rec	n1–3	slur	S; no slur RW
	bc	n2	♯	RW
		n3	no fig	RW
m57	bc	n1–2	no fig	RW

Third movement

m3	bc	n1	6/4 3/♭	RW
		n2	no fig	RW
m3–4	bc		no tie	RSW
m4	bc	n1	♭	RW
m4–5	rec		no tie	RW
m6	rec	n1–2	slur	S
	bc	n2	5/4/♮	RW
m7	bc	n1	no fig	RW
m9–10	bc		no tie	RW

Fourth movement

m1	rec	n2–3	[♩. ♪]	RSW; slur S
		n5–6	quaver d′′	RSW
m2	rec	n2	no tr	RW
m5	rec	n3	no tr	RW
m6	bc	n1	5	RW
m7	bc	n5	no fig	RW
		n7	no fig	RW

m8	bc	n1	5	*RW*
m10	rec	n3–4	no slur	*RW*
		n5–6	no slur	*RW*
m11	rec	n2	*tr*	*S*
m12	bc	n8	no fig	*RW*
m14	rec	n1–2	no slur	*RSW*
		n3–4	no slur	*RSW*
m18	bc	n1	no fig	*RW*
		n3	no fig	*RW*
m20	bc	n3	5	*RW*
m25	rec		no app	*RW*; quaver app *S*
m26	rec	n2–3	♩. ♫	*RSW*
		n4	*tr*	*S*
		n5–6	quaver d″	*RSW*
m29	bc	n5	no fig	*RW*
		n7	no fig	*RW*
m31	rec	n2	*tr*	*RW*
m33	bc	n1	6/4	*RW*
		n3	5/♯	*RW*

A minor Sonata

First movement

Grave	R			
Andante	S			
m2	bc	n1	𝄽	*RW*
		n3	no fig	*RW*
		n5	no fig	*RW*
m5	rec	n1	*tr*	*RSW*
m6	bc	n1–2	♫	*S*
m10	bc	n1	𝄽	*RW*
		n3	no fig	*RW*
		n5	6/4	*S*
m11	bc	n1	6	*RSW*
		n5	6/4	*RW*; no fig *S*
m12	bc	n1	no fig	*RW*; 6 *S*
		n3	no fig	*RSW*
m15	bc	n1	no fig	*RW*
		n3	no fig	*RW*
m17	bc	n1	6	*RW*; no fig *S*
		n3	no fig	*RW*
m19	bc	n1	7	*RW*
m20	bc	n3	no fig	*RW*
m21	rec	n5	*tr*	*RSW*
m24	rec	n1–2	♩. ♪	*RSW*
		n4	b″	*RSW*
m25	rec	n1–2	♩. ♪	*RSW*
		n3–4	♫	*RSW*
m26	rec	n1–2	♩. ♪	*RSW*
		n3–4	♫	*S*
	bc	n7	♯ missing on C	*RSW*
m28	rec	n1–2	♫	*RSW*
m31	bc	n1	5	*RW*
		n5	no fig	*RSW*
m32	rec	n1–2	♫	*RSW*
m33	bc	n1–4	♫♫	*RW*
		n1	no fig	*S*
		n3	no fig	*S*

m34	rec	n1–2	♩. ♪	*RSW*
m35	rec	n4	*tr*	*RSW*
	bc	n2	♯	*R*
		n3	no fig	*R*
m36	bc	n1	no fig	*RS*
m38	bc	n7	F°♯	*RSW*
m39	rec	n1–2	♩. ♪	*RSW*
		n3–4	♫	*RSW*
	bc	n6	𝄽	*W*
m40	rec	n3–4	♫	*S*
m42	rec	n1–2	no tie	*S*
m44	rec		no tie	*S*
	bc	n7	𝄽	*RW*; no fig *S*
m46	bc	n3	4	*S*
		n4	♯	*RSW*
m47	rec	n1–2	♩. ♪	*RSW*
		n3–4	♫	*S*
m48	rec	n4–5	♩. ♪	*RSW*
m49	rec	n1–2	♩. ♪	*RSW*
		n3	*tr*	*RSW*
		n3–4	♩. 𝄾 ♪	*W*
	Adagio absent			*MRS*

Second movement

m6	bc	n1	5	*RW*
m9	bc	n3	6	*RW*; no fig *S*
		n4	no fig	*RW*
m10	rec	n1–2	no slur	*RSW*
		n3	*tr*	*RSW*
m18	rec	n3–5	♫ e″ c″	*RSW*
	bc	n9	6	*RW*; no fig *S*
m19	rec	n2	*tr*	*RSW*
m20	bc	n9–11	E° C° E°	*MRSW*
m21	rec	n6	♯ missing	*S*
	bc	n1	6	*RW*
		n3	no fig	*RSW*
		n4	♯	*RSW*
m25	bc	n5	no fig	*RW*
m26	bc	n5	5	*RW*
m27	rec	n4	*tr*	*RSW*
	bc	n3	♯	*RW*
m29	rec	n2–3	no tie	*RSW*
m30	rec	n4	*tr*	*RSW*
m34	bc	n5	no fig	*RW*
		n14	B°	*RSW*; 𝄽/5♮ *S*
m37	bc	n2	6	*RW*
		n3	6	*RW*; no fig *S*
		n4	no fig	*RW*
m38	rec	n1–2	crotchet c″	*RSW*

Third movement

Largo	S			
m1	rec	n3	b′♭	*RW*
		n4	dotted crotchet	*RSW*
	bc	n2	no fig	*RW*
m2	rec	n2–3	♩. ♬	*RSW*
		n6–8	♬ (tr)	*RSW*
m4	rec	n1	no *tr*	*S*

77

m4	rec	n4–5	tie	RSW
		n5	no *tr*	S
		n7–10	[note figure]	RW
		n8–10	[note figure]	S
	bc	n3	no fig	RSW
		n4	♭	RSW
		n7	no fig	RSW
m5	rec	n6–8	no slur	MR
	bc	n3	♭	RSW
m6	rec	n2–4	no slur	S
		n6–7	[note figure]	RSW
		n10–12	no slur	S
m8	rec	n10	*tr*	RSW
m9	rec	n5	*tr*	RSW
m12	bc	n4	no fig	RSW
m15	rec	n1	[dotted note]	RSW
		n5	*tr*	RW
	bc	n1	[dotted note]	RSW
m16		n5	Adagio	RS

Fourth movement

m6	rec	n5	d''	RSW
	bc	n1	6	RSW
m7	bc	n1	6	RSW
		n6–8	6	RSW
m8	bc	n2–4	6	RSW
		n6–8	6	RSW
m9	bc	n6	6	RSW
		n8	6	RSW
m13	bc	n4	7/♯	RW
		n6	2	RW
m14	bc	n2	7/♯	RW
m15	rec	n5–6	tie	RSW
m16	bc	n2	6	RSW
m18	bc	n3	crotchet rest	RS
m20	bc	rest after n8	no fig	RSW
		n9	5	RW
m22	bc	n3–4	6	RSW
		n5	[symbol]	RW
		n6	no fig	RW
m24	rec	n2	*tr*	RSW
m31	bc	n3–4	6	RSW
		n5	6♭	RW
m32	bc	n2	6	RSW
		n3	6♭	RW
m33	rec	n2–4	no slur	RS
	bc	n6	6/5	RSW
m35	rec	n5–7	[note figure]	W
m36	bc	n4	no fig	RW
m37	bc	n6	7	RSW
		n7	7/♯	RSW
		n8	[symbol]	RSW
m40	bc	n1	4 3	RSW
		n2	no fig	RSW
m41	bc	n1	4 3	RSW
		n3	no fig	RSW
		n4	6	RSW

m41	bc	n5	no fig	RSW
		n6	6	RSW
m42	bc	n8	6	RSW
m44	bc	n7	6♭	RSW
m45	bc	n5	6	RSW
m46	bc	n5	no fig	RSW
m48	bc	n3	6♭	RSW
		n4–5	6	RSW
m49	rec	n1	*tr*	RSW

C major Sonata

First movement

m6	bc	n4–5	no fig	S
m8	rec	n2–4	no slur	R
m9	rec	n6–8	[note figure]	RW
m10	bc	n1	no fig	A
		n2	no fig	AS
m13	rec	n2–4	no slur	AS
m21	rec	n11–13	[note figure]	RW

Second movement

m29	bc	n3	e^0	RW
m38	rec	n1	*tr*	S
m44	rec		no tie	RW
m71	rec	n2	*tr*	RW
m82	bc	n1	no fig	ARSW
m90	bc	n1	no fig	ARSW
m92	bc	n1	no fig	RW
		n5	no fig	RW
m93	bc	n5	no fig	ARSW
m110	bc	n1–2	no fig	RW
m130	rec		*tr* on n2	RW

Third movement

Adagio		G major flute sonata		
Andante		F major oboe sonata		
m28	bc	n2	no fig	RW; 4 S
m32	rec	n2–4	slur	cf G major flute sonata

Fourth movement
Absent in *R*

A tempo di Gavotti				W
a tempo di Gavotto				AS
m15	rec	n5	no *tr*	AW
m29	bc	n3	♮/♯	W; ♯/4 A

Fifth movement

m2	rec	n1–2	no strokes	RW
m4	rec	n1–2	no strokes	AM; staccato dots RW
m5	rec	n1–2	staccato dots	RW
m27	bc	n1	no fig	RSW
m31	rec	n1	*tr*	RSW
m36	rec	n1	no *tr*	ARSW
m44	rec	n1	no *tr*	RW
m54	rec	n1–3	no slur	AR

F major Sonata

First movement

Grave — *M*
(Larghetto — *ARSW* and organ concerto)

m		note		source
m28	rec	n1–2	[notation]	*ARSW*
		n3	*tr*	*ARSW*
		n5	*tr*	*ARSW*
m42	rec	n2–3	[notation]	*ARSW*
m43	rec	n1–2	[notation]	*ARSW*

Second movement

¢ — *S*

m		note		source
m3	rec	n5	*tr*	*RSW*
m4	bc	n2	6	*ARSW*
		n8	6/5	*RW*
m5	rec	n4–5	[notation] c'' e''	*ARSW*
	bc	n2	no fig	*ARSW*
m9	bc	n1	6	*ARSW*
m16	bc	n4	6/♭	*RSW*
m17	bc	n4	f°♯, no fig	*RSW*
m23	bc	n3–4	no fig	*ARSW*
m24	rec	n8	*tr*	*ARSW*
m25	rec	n4	*tr*	*RSW*

Third movement

Siciliana — *RSW*

m		note		source
m4	rec	n1–2	no slur	*ARSW*
m5	rec	n1–2	no slur	*ARSW*
m6	bc	n1	5	*RW*
m7	rec	n4	d''	*ARSW*
m8	rec	n4	*tr*	*RSW*
	bc	n5	no fig	*RSW*
m9	bc	n2	6	*R*; no fig *AS*
		n6	6	*RSW*; no fig *A*
m10	rec	n4–5	no slur	*ARSW*
		n9	*tr*	*AW*

Fourth movement

m		note		source
m13	rec	n9	no tie	*ARSW*
m14	rec	n1	crotchet rest	*ARSW*
		n2–4	quaver b''	*ARSW*
		n5	[dotted crotchet]	*ARSW*
		n6–8	quaver b''	*ARSW*
m19	rec	n1–2	d''' c'''	*ARSW*
	bc	n1	no fig	*ARSW*
m27	bc	n6	6	*ARSW*
		n7	no fig	*ARSW*

B♭ major Sonata

First movement

For tempo marking cf Overture to *Scipione*

Second movement

m		note		
m8	rec	n2–4	[notation]	but cf organ concerto

Third movement

m		note		
m9	rec	n2–5	} [notation]	
		n7–10	}	
m10	rec	n2–5		
m30	rec	n2–5		

m		note		
m30	rec	n7–10	[notation]	
m31	rec	n1	a'	but cf violin sonata (and by analogy with m9–10 & 30)
		n2–5	[notation]	

D minor Sonata

First movement

m		note		source
m4	bc	n4–5	[notation]	*M*
m7	rec	n10	no *tr*	*M*
m8	rec	n8–12	slur	*M*
		n9–12	slur	*RSW*; no slur *A*
	bc	n4	no fig	*ARW*
m9	rec	n2	♭ missing	*M*
		n2–3	[notation]	*RW*
m10	bc	n1	♯	*RW*
		n7–8	4 ♯	*RW*
m12	bc	n2	no fig	*RW*
m13	rec	n1	*tr*	*M*
m14	bc	n5	no fig	*MS*
m15	rec	n1	no *tr*	*AS*
	bc	n5	no fig	*MS*
m17	rec	n8	no *tr*	*RSW*
m19	rec	n3	no *tr*	*AM*

Bass octave higher in *RW*: m6 n7–9, m7, m8 n1–2

Second movement

m		note		source
m1	rec	n1–2	strokes	*AS*
m4	rec	n4	no *tr*	*RSW*
m5	rec	n1–3	no slur	*M*

and continuing throughout the movement in *M* and sometimes *AS*

m		note		source
m12	rec	n3	no *tr*	*MRW*
m24	rec	n3	no *tr*	*M*
m27	rec	n4	no *tr*	*M*
m33	bc	n1	6	*AMS*
m36	bc	n4	e°♭	*S*
m37	bc	n1	e°♭	*S*
m42	bc	n2	4	*RW*

Bass octave higher in *RW*: m42

Third movement

Furioso — *M*
¢ — *RW*

m		note		source
m3	bc	n1	no fig	*RW*
		n3	no fig	*RSW*
		n12	e'♮	*M*
m10	bc	n4	no fig	*M*
m11	bc	n1, 3, 5, 7 9, 11, 13	no fig	*M*
m12	bc	n2–4	no fig	*M*
m14	bc	n12	no fig	*RW*
m18	rec	n2	no *tr*	*RSW*
	bc	n5	e'♮	*M*
m22	bc	n1	6	*M*
		n8	e°♮	*S*
m23	rec	n1	no *tr*	*ARSW*
m27	bc	n5	6	*M*

m27	bc	n7	no fig	M
		n9	6	M
		n11	no fig	M
m28	rec	n6	f″	AMS
	bc	n1	6	M
		n3	no fig	M
		n5	6	M
		n7	no fig	M
		n9	♮/6	M
		n11	no fig	M
		n13	6	M
		n15	no fig	M
m29	bc	n1	6	M
		n3	no fig	M
		n5	6	M
		n7	no fig	M
		n11	no fig	M
m33	bc	n4	6	M

Bass octave higher in *RW*: m14, m15 n1

Bass octave lower in *RW*: m12 n5

Fourth movement

m2	bc	n4	no fig	ARSW
m5	rec	n2	no *tr*	S
m9	rec	n1–2	[music]	RW
m19	rec	n1–3	no slur	RW

Bass octave higher in *RW*: m13

Fifth movement

m6	bc	n3	♯	RW
m22	rec		no *tr*	ARSW
m28	bc	n1	♯	RW
m33	rec		no *tr*	RSW
m37	bc	n3	no fig	RW
m43	bc	n1	7/5	RW
m61	bc	n3	♯	RW
m76	bc		semibreve rest	RSW
m83–4	rec		no tie	RW
m93			absent	M
m94	bc		7♮	RW
m96			absent	AM
m97			absent	AM

Bass octave higher in *RW*: m22–m28 n2; m57 n2–m63 n2

Sixth movement

No tempo marking				M
m2	rec	n8	b″	M; f″ W
	bc	n8	no fig	W
m3	rec	n1–7	[music]	M
	bc	n1	f°, 6	M
m4	bc	n8	6/5	R
m5	rec	n1–7	[music]	M
	bc	n1	a°, 6	M
		n2	no fig	W
m7	rec	n7	no tie	W
	bc	n2	no fig	ARSW
		n4	no fig	ARSW

m8	rec	n2–3	f″ g″	M
		n4	no *tr*	M
	bc	n2	B°	RS
m10	bc	n5	no fig	W
m11	bc	n2	♯	MW
		n5	♯	AMW
m12	rec	n1	d″	W
		n7	♩.	R
	bc	n4	♯	W
		n8	no fig	W
m13	rec	n1–7	[music]	M
	bc	n4	♯	RW
m18	bc	n5	no fig	W
		n8	no fig	W
m19	bc	n5	no fig	ASW
m20	bc	n4	♯	W

Bass octave higher in *R*: m13 n2–4

Seventh movement

A tempo di Minuet				ARW
No tempo marking				M2
3/8 (but barred in 6/8)				M2
m1	rec	n1–3	no slur	M
	bc	n3	6	M
m5	rec	n3	no *tr*	MRSW
	bc	n2	6	M
m6	bc	n4	6	RW
		n6	6	RW
m7	rec	n1–2	no slur	MM2RW
		n3	no *tr*	M
	bc	n6	no fig	RW
m8	rec	n1–2	no slur	AMM2RW
		n3	no *tr*	MM2
m9	bc	n1	no fig	M
m11	bc	n5	♯	AM2RSW
m12	rec	rest before	tied a″	
		n1	semiquaver	MM2
		n2–3	[music]	M2
	bc	n2	no fig	M2; 4 RW
m19	rec	n3	no *tr*	RW
m20	rec	n1–3	[music]	M2

Early version of sixth movement

m9	rec	n4–6	[music]	